Rest In Ink

Unraveling the Mysteries Behind Every Word

Aditi Pant

India | USA | UK

Made with ❤ on the BookLeaf Publishing Platform

www.bookleafpub.in

www.bookleafpub.com

Dedication

I dedicate this collection to YOU

Preface

In "Rest in Ink," I delve into the familiar yet profound thoughts that have shaped my understanding of life since childhood. This collection reflects my journey through moments of joy, sorrow, and introspection, serving as a canvas for my reflections on the world around me. The loss of my father and uncle, along with various academic and personal setbacks, triggered a cascade of questions about existence, purpose, and the nature of life and death. These experiences stirred in me a deep desire to explore not only my feelings but also the underlying truths of our shared human experience.

Growing up in a family enriched by diverse intellectual pursuits—my father, a Branch Manager at a Regional Rural Bank; my mother, a passionate reader and PhD in Hindi literature who recently retired as Dean of her college; and my brother, an IIT Delhi graduate with a curiosity for engineering—I often found myself pondering the dynamics of our unique family and the people surrounding me. This environment, filled with both good friendships and wayward acquaintances, led me to reflect deeply on my connections and experiences, prompting me to ask questions about why I was surrounded by the people I was and how they shaped my identity.

To make sense of my feelings and observations, I began writing letters & poems—random, heartfelt messages to the universe, nature, and even to myself. Each letter became a way to confront my uncertainties, celebrate my joys, and articulate the myriad emotions accompanying my journey. As I navigated the complexities of life, my experiences and the way I reacted to my curiosities began to evolve. I found that as I developed into a better version of myself, the tone and content of these letters also transformed, reflecting my growth as a person.

Every poem in this collection resonates with a universal quality that readers will find relatable. Each one captures emotions that many have felt —be it joy, sorrow, confusion, or introspection— inviting readers to see their own experiences mirrored in my words. "Rest in Ink" captures this intimate dialogue, encouraging readers to explore the questions we all grapple with about life, loss, and the intricate mosaics of relationships that define our existence. Through this collection, I hope to resonate with anyone who has ever questioned their path, sought solace in written words, or yearned for connection in a world filled with uncertainty.

-Aditi Pant

Acknowledgements

To my mother, Dr. Alka Pant, and my father, Late Mahesh Chandra Pant, for gifting me with the most precious inheritance of all — the writer's genes. You both passed on the creativity, the words, and, let's be honest, probably the endless 'chatter' that made you question your life choices at least once (or twice). Your constant support, boundless wisdom, and relentless encouragement have shaped me into who I am today — and, no doubt, kept me from writing some *very* questionable "experimental" short stories. Thank you for being my first editors, my harshest critics, and my most devoted cheerleaders. Without you, I'd still be trying to figure out how to string two sentences together.

To my brother, Aditya Pant (Bhaiya), and his wonderful fiancée, Megha Anand, for being my partners in crime, my biggest cheerleaders, and the best distractions when life feels a little too serious. Bhaiya, your endless patience, sense of humor, and ability to keep me grounded have always been my anchor. And Megha, thank you for bringing even more joy and warmth into our family. You both make life so much brighter!

To my life partner, CS Midhasaya Purohit, whose love is both a quiet strength and a fierce fire that keeps me going. You've been my sanctuary in a world full of chaos, my unwavering support when the path felt unclear, and the reason I keep believing in myself, even on the toughest days. Your patience has been a silent comfort, your belief in me a constant reminder of what I'm capable of. You've seen me at my most vulnerable, yet you've always loved me harder in those moments. Thank you for being the person who holds my heart so tenderly and fiercely at once. In you, I've found not just a partner, but the home I never knew I was searching for.

To my father-in-law, mother-in-law and Nani, for showing me what it truly means to break stereotypes and embrace a love that doesn't confine me to any norms. Your acceptance, encouragement, and belief in me have given me the space to shine in ways I never imagined possible. You've created a world where I could be myself — not just as a daughter-in-law, but as a person with dreams and aspirations. The way you have loved and supported me, without judgment or limitation, is a gift I will always treasure. Thank you for being the pillars of strength and wisdom who helped me grow, and for allowing me to flourish in my own light.

To my constant, Sahil Sharma (Hilsa Machli), for being my rock, my laughter, and the one who understands me without a single word needing to be said. You are the calm in my storms, the warmth in my coldest moments, and the person who always knows how to make me smile. Thank you for being the steady presence in my life — my greatest support, and my heart's home.

To my confidants: Harshila (Kunnu), Gursimran (Guru), and Ayushi (Ballu) — words can never quite capture how deeply grateful I am for you. You've been my safe space, my sounding boards, and the ones who've understood me without needing any explanations. Through every joy, every tear, and every moment of doubt, you've been right there — not just listening, but feeling it all with me. Thank you for being my constants in a world that changes too fast, for sharing both the quiet moments and the loud ones. You are the family I choose, and I'm so lucky to have you by my side.

And to all my friends and family members, whose love and faith have made every word I write possible. This book is as much yours as it is mine.

1. I welcome you death!

Finally you are here,
Finally you are near.
So divine and strong,
So pure and clear.

No hidden mysteries,
No buried secrets.
No more turning back,
No more awaiting concepts.

He said turn back one more time,
One more time rewind and refine.
From here there is no turning back
There is no walking ahead.

I felt the cold in his blue eyes,
I felt the warmth in his blooded eyes.
Surprised and amused,
Pushed against the wall,
I was left with no way.

Confused, happy, sad and still,
Blocking my path were these devils.
No I said leave me and let me feel,

Let me feel the confused happiness,
Let me feel the still sadness.

Suddenly moving,
Everything running so fast
I can hear sum one at distance weeping so loud.
I turned back and saw, Oh! It was not me,
It was not me, for whom they are sad,
He is someone else and yes I am glad.

I am glad coz I am now free,
No more joys, no more worries.
No more obligations, no more pleas.
No more fear and sorrows of detachments,
No more joys and happiness of attachments.

Above all now I am who I am,
No outline, no norm,
No guilt, no form.
Above from further ends,
Above from dead ends,
Above from fear of sinking and burning thoughts,
Above from split and re-joining thoughts,
Now everything is black,
With open arms I welcome you death.

2. Endless Echoes

Every moment,
I am alone.
The trickling sound,
keep pouring.
Above all thoughts and illusions,
I create my own form.
I break it repeatedly,
And lose myself again and again.
Like a flame, every moment,
I burn.
I hope the rays of my dreams will show a better way.
Why do I build such bridges?

Every moment,
I am alone.
The trickling sound,
Keep pouring.
The point is the same,
The essence remains unchanged,
Like zero —
Endless, yet empty.
Like the holes,
I try to fill their cracks.
It is deep and profound,

Unyielding and rare,
It is very bitter,
Yet still, I narrate that story.

Every moment,
I am alone.
The trickling sound,
Keep pouring.
When the clouds rain,
They become light.
Lighter than clouds,
They become water.
Drenched in water,
They are like scraps of paper,
Every day, I burn them,
Even though they never cool down.
Where will I offer them for purification?
The embers still burn somewhere,
Why should I offer them to you?

Every moment,
I am alone.
The trickling sound,
Just keep pouring...

3. The Keeper of Our Nights

The big yellowish ball,
Hiding the secrets of soul.
Peeping into the hearts,
Through the giant windows.

Few blessed with rays so divine,
Few cursed with doomed shines.
Faded beauty but so real,
Glittering more in the shores of Rhine.

With every falling beam,
I feel the flood;
Pouring down the nectar,
Soaked in the heated blood.

But above, the moon watches,
a silent sentinel of the night,
bearing witness to laughter,
to tears, to whispered confessions.

It holds the weight of our joys,
the echoes of our fights,
a luminous observer,
in the vastness of the dark.

It glimmers on rooftops,
dances on the water's edge,
as celebrations unfold
and arguments flare.

Yet it keeps its counsel,
unravelling stories in soft light,
a guardian of secrets
etched in the stars.

As dawn approaches,
the moon begins to fade,
slipping away gently,
leaving whispers behind.

It bows to the sun,
the big yellowish ball,
a cycle of surrender,
a promise to return,
ever watchful, ever silent,
the keeper of our nights.

4. The Mystical Maze: An Illusion

What is this illusion you weave,
How did you craft this form, believe.
Unique, distinct, yet all the same,
Different yet familiar, no one to blame.

Shape and color, so apart,
But nature varies in every heart.
Yet, beneath it all, a shadow stays,
How did you shape this wondrous maze?

You gave us power with birth's embrace,
Bound our breath in one sacred space,
But death's dominion you did not bestow,
What a conspiracy, what a show.

You gave joy, you gave sorrow,
A path to reveal, a road to follow.
In endless dark, a light would gleam,
A beacon in night's vast, silent dream.

This twisted riddle, you divided so,
One who understood, would rise and glow.
The rest would falter, lost in the haze,

What is this illusion, this mystic maze?

8

5. Whispers of the Shattered Self

Who am I, what am I,
Troubled by the essence of my own sigh.
I am happy, I am sad,
Lost in my emotions, feeling so bad.

You teach me life again and again,
You make me cry, inflict this pain,
I'm troubled by the turmoil of my fate,
Caught in the struggle, it's too late.

It never feels complete, will it ever be so?
What I've lost, will it ever return to grow?
I'm weary of this battle, the give and the take,
Trapped in the turmoil of what I forsake.

I've prayed a thousand times,
Hoping for solace, hoping for signs,
But I'm troubled by this ritual of repeating,
Each prayer, each plea, constantly defeating.

My circumstances, my foes remain the same,
Words that sting, always to blame.
Nothing has changed, all has fallen apart,

I'm left with the pieces of a broken heart.

I'm troubled by the fragments of a letter once whole,
The broken remnants, the ache in my soul.

6. The Refuge of Quiet Grace

This is a home, a place of peace,
A light for those whose spirits cease.
Away from struggle, free from care,
Unaware of burdens, it's always fair.

It hums a lullaby, it scolds sometimes,
It speaks its own language, in its rhymes.
This is a home, a place of peace,
A light for those whose spirits cease.

Between the dark and the light it plays,
Sometimes dirty, it weeps for its days,
It cares for itself with quiet grace.

It hides things here and there with haste,
A million secrets it holds in place,
Never speaks a word, but with emotions, it's wise,
It honors feelings, never denies.

This is a home, a place of peace,
A light for those whose spirits cease.
It changes form a thousand times,
Adapting to life, flowing with time,

Living with people, dying with them too,
It offers a refuge for all to renew.

This tiny life, it finds its way,
For it too has work, come what may.
This is a home, a place of peace,
A light for those whose spirits cease.

7. Beneath the Veil of Time

My innocent smile, now a fleeting grin,
Sadness turned to anger deep within.

With time, small desires became needs,
Have I really grown this much indeed?

The tangles in my hair, now styled with care,
Freedom turned to responsibility, unaware.

The playful acts of childhood now behind,
Have I truly grown, leaving it all behind?

My words now louder than theirs,
My habits, in contrast, unaware.

The lap where I once played with glee,
Is it smaller now, or have I truly grown, you see?

8. The Dance of Endurance

Amidst the smoke and the chaos, she emerges,
Flowing, shouting, as her spirit surges.

Sometimes laughing, sometimes bearing in sorrow,
She speaks to all, of a hope for tomorrow.

For comfort, she leans on fleeting delight,
But under the weight, she hides from the light.

Amidst the storms, like a flame, she seeks peace,
Hoping for calm, a sweet release.

Falling, rising, again and again,
She clings to life, through joy and pain.

Witnessing the trials, yet with a smile,
She grins within, enduring all the while.

She asks, is this life's true call?
Yes, this is life, standing tall.

9. Shadows of the Abandoned

That old house still feels haunting,
As if it's hiding past tragedies, still daunting.

The walls' colors, its shadows, now faint,
Yet its gaze remains fixed, where the doorways await.

The footprints in the courtyard, now erased,
All the flowers and leaves, withered and laid to rest in
haste.

No one now dares to peek inside,
Perhaps the house still waits, for someone to arrive.

10. Threads of the Same Cloth

How alike we seem, like reflections in a glass,
Is our name and faith perhaps one, steadfast?

Our habits and words so closely entwine,
Could our paths to destiny be one, by design?

Your touch feels so familiar, so deeply known,
Are our fingerprints perhaps one, not alone?

Before you ask of my faith, my friend so true,
Look first at our blood, is its color not one too?

11. Beyond Time, Beyond All

There are millions like me in your world,
But I have only one, and that is you— my truth unfurled.

In a crowd of faces, none carry your light,
Each glance you offer pulls me from the night.

You have countless reasons to embrace joy's grace,
Yet I need no more than your presence, your trace.

In your laughter, I find a quiet, lasting ease,
A stillness that speaks, a deep, timeless peace.

Around you, a hundred hopes may circle, near,
But my only hope, my singular wish, is that you stay
here.

Through both calm and chaos, you are my steady guide,
A constant, a flame that neither flickers nor hides.

Your moments reach into countless tomorrows,
But mine are bound by you— the one constant, through
all sorrows.

In your presence, time loses its grasp,
For in your love, I find all I seek, all I have.

18

12. The Flow of Life

It is not in the nature to chase something or someone,
It is the attitude we grow, the gesture we've won.
A lifetime given, a sacrifice made,
To unwind the truth, through time's steady fade.

You bring out a different face of me,
And in return, I promise, I'll set you free.
I promise to initiate, with heart and with mind.
Do not take that chance from me, please, be kind.

I do not know the purpose of this life we hold,
The reason for resistance, or what it's meant to unfold.
I am living—just living, the 24 hours given to me,
Enjoying each moment, as pure as can be.

Sharing my gift with all the souls I meet,
Form nowhere you appeared, and eternity felt complete.
An eternal bond with an immortal soul,
The outline of life, a journey to make us whole.

We act, we react, searching for our own,
And in this search, the perfect soul is known.
There is nothing to hide, we see and we share,
What others have, we crave, unaware.

What we have, others seek with longing eyes,
For we are all reflections, beneath the same skies.
Chasing shadows, yet finding no truth to bind,
In the end, it's ourselves we seek to find.

Take my glasses and peer through their lens,
You've given enough; let your aura transcend.
Do not let guilt, nor scar, mark your heart,
For what you've done, is a work of art.

The pain of loss isn't in pounds or weight,
It's in the bonds that we hesitate to create.
People around you will take the storms,
Strength isn't bought—it's built through storms.

Uncertainty gives way to opportunities new,
A path that leads to certainties, shining through.
Our responsibility, to not get trapped in strife,
But to live, learn, grow, and embrace this life.

Come what may, the pieces fall as they must,
We learn to flow, in them we trust.
Not everyone in this world is free enough to ask,
To dig the roots and plant the grass.

The grass of hope, of love, of light,

The grass of care, and smiles so bright.
The grass of freedom, of life to shine,
A gift of nature, let it flow divine.

This life is a gift, don't let it decay,
Let it flow naturally, in its own way.

13. Counting the Running Colours!

For the sake of joy, and through endless miles,
I confess, I am selfish, drawn by your tender smile.

Counting each step, yet lost in infinity's embrace,
Helpless, I stand, before fate's unyielding face.

Many reasons may arise, some fading, some dying,
Lost in the brilliance, where their whispers go quiet,
sighing.

I wait for the marigold to bloom anew,
To unfurl its vibrant petals, and heal the ache I pursue.

I dissolve myself, taking the shape of another,
For in their form, I seek to rediscover.

Chasing the rainbow, with colors running wild,
Endlessly counting hues, like a restless child.

Through every fleeting moment, I chase the light,
As it shifts and dances, in the depths of the night.

In this pursuit, I lose and find myself once more,

An endless journey, with each color I adore.

14. Owed to You

Chilling heat, the air so dry,
Bleary eyes beneath the sky,
A touch that stirs, a sudden surprise,
Unlocking treasures, beyond the guise.

The world unfolds, a mystery deep,
In nature's arms, where secrets sleep.
Hunting for more, with yearning so pure,
A restless spirit, seeking a cure.

Satisfied, yet mesmerized by the view,
Wondering how this all came true.
Was it a decision, made on a whim,
Or the perfect moment, when stars align within?

Summing it up, cutting the ends,
Finishing tasks, as the time bends.
Each errand tangled, now undone,
The journey complete, but the story's just begun.

I owe you the success, the road that was paved,
I owe you the joy, from the risks we both braved.
I owe you this life, this love intertwined,
A life lived in disguise, with you by my side.

Through shadows and light, we've made our way,
With you, my guide, I've learned how to stay.
For all that we've shared, the truth remains clear,
I owe you my life, and all I hold dear.

15. Eternal Fire

Not having you did not make my love less,
No bundle of words could ever express.
You are the sky, so vast and so wide,
And though I cannot touch you, you are always by my
side.

Someday, the world will stand still,
All painted in hues of blue and grey, time to fulfill.
Lie beside me, under the endless sky,
Beneath the stars where our spirits fly.

The horizon stretches with peace and grace,
And in that stillness, I find your face.
In the quiet, see there you are,
No distance between us, no matter how far.

Sink with me in the broken, beautiful things,
In the moments where time itself clings.
Skip the eternities when we were apart,
For now we are together, heart to heart.

See the beauty in the fire that ignites,
Two souls entwined, burning through nights.
They do not search for light, for it's already found,

Their friction pure, with love profound.

Their love burns bright, like stars in the sky,
Unfading, unbroken, it will never die.
For in each other, they find their spark,
A fire eternal, lighting the dark.

16. A Choice in Eternity

A letter to him from her;
With love and fear, her heart a blur.
Choosing the same you, over and over,
In each moment, I draw nearer, I hover.

I convince myself, though doubt may creep,
That in you, my soul will forever keep.
I convince others, with words so sweet,
For the sake of mortality, for the answer I seek.

Look at the beauty, within your eyes,
Where the stars in the darkness rise.
Hidden deep, like a secret untold,
A quiet warmth, a love so bold.

Search for the sanctity that lies inside,
Where hope and faith in silence collide.
Search for it, where it softly resides,
In the places where time itself abides.

For I know, deep within my heart,
That we are bound, though worlds may part.
In every breath, in every tear,
I choose you, year after year.

Though fear may linger, love will remain,
Through joy, through sorrow, through every pain.
For in you, I've found my truth and grace,
A love eternal, no time can erase.

But here lies the truth, with hands held high,
I give myself to you, and to God, I rely.
For love requires sacrifice, a soul's deep surrender,
To the divine, to the light, to love's pure center.

So I lay down my heart, my dreams, my might,
Offering all, in the stillness of night.
For in giving myself, I am set free,
Bound to you, yet bound to eternity.

So here, in this letter, I bare my soul,
A plea, a promise, to make me whole.
For the sake of us, for the sake of now,
I choose you, forever, no matter how.

And in this choice, I give up my own,
To walk beside you, but never alone.
For in God's embrace, we find our way,
Together, in love, for all of our days.

17. In This Sacred Space

Your glimpse—a fleeting spark,
In the stairwell's breath, a quiet arc.
The room holds its breath,
As you, like a dream, softly glide,
With the holy scent, like incense, abloom,
Filling the air where shadows loom.

We, two indices, touch at the edge,
Each carrying stories, a sacred pledge.
Yours different from mine, yet aligned,
In love's embrace, tenderly twined.

Through crowded whispers and noisy din,
Your arms, like a haven, pull me in.
Burning darker, under starless skies,
Where the weight of silence amplifies.

Deep within, where the battle brews,
In the realm of black and blue.
Yet, in the quiet, all becomes true—
When it's just me and you.

The storm may rage, the world may fall,
But here, within your touch, I stand tall.

Through the wars we fight, beneath the moon,
In the shelter of our hearts, we're immune.

A game of shadows, a dance of grace,
When it's just me and you in this sacred space.

18. Whispers in the Desert

Spaces sought, where silence lingers,
Whispered in shadows, through trembling fingers.
Spaces given, like breaths in between,
Under creases, where secrets convene.

A world folded softly, an intricate maze,
Where something—unsaid—quietly stays.
Clues and blues weave through the air,
A curtain of longing, with hints of despair.

Blurred demarcations, where lines fade away,
Like dreams lost in the stillness of day.

Flying high, with wings unearned,
Beneath the weight of hopes unturned,
Void of expectations, silent cries,
Tethered to the heavens, yet bound to the skies.

Every time, time was given,
A currency spent, a wayward rhythm driven.
Each time, reasons were offered,
Like soft songs that never quite hovered.

Am I the oasis in a barren land?

The only whisper, the only hand?
Am I the one who dares to believe,
In a world that asks, yet never receives?

In the desert of doubt, where shadows roam,
Is my heart the only place I can call home?
Am I the lone echo in a hollowed void,
The last breath of hope, quietly employed?
Will I be convinced, or left adrift,
In the spaces sought, where truths shift?

19. The Free Soul

The free soul;
Sublime in its nature.
Standing nowhere;
Present everywhere.
Standing again at zero miles;
Floating with the thoughts;
Hovering over the mob.

The free soul;
Like an open book;
Open for the thoughts.
Like a canvas;
Open for the mocks.

The free soul;
Whistling with the life.
With every turn;
Reminds to thrive.

Moving ahead
From dark to light.
Tracks reflecting the nature;
Nature reflecting the light.

The free soul
Feels the passing day.
Growing with me;
The stains of love;
Fill the day.

Then why the Soul is thirsty?
Wandering in search.

Again the real is unreal;
Again the nature is partial.
Lotus blooms with unseen bells;
It's nothing but the journey to oneself...

20. Through Time and Silence

In the blues
I will wait for You

With the yellow impressions
I will get darker in the memories

We will meet again and again
Always destined to be...

In the horizon
With one left and one right

Leaving the marks
With one wrong and one right...

Oh! Dear
We were always there
In each other
In some form or other...

21. Awaiting the Ashes

The red deamoned eyes;
Waiting for the catch.

Furnace opened;
With the heat so high.

Marks of burns;
Were still fresh;
Oh! Here it comes;
The another flesh.

I am waiting here,
With all my eyes on road.

Lashes are burning,
With the heated sours.

Wait you poor! Wait
Have faith and notice
the changing shapes.

I will wait
I promise to wait
To remake the grounds laid

Till the edges finally fade...

38

www.ingramcontent.com/pod-product-compliance
Lightning Source LLC
LaVergne TN
LVHW021304200726
843509LV00012B/1771